WHITTIER: A PICTURE POSTCARD HISTORY

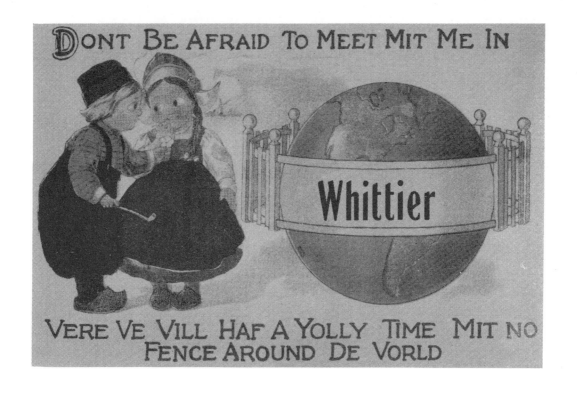

DONT BE AFRAID TO MEET MIT ME IN

Whittier

VERE VE VILL HAF A YOLLY TIME MIT NO
FENCE AROUND DE VORLD

WHITTIER

A PICTURE POSTCARD HISTORY

by

RUDY VALDEZ

MONDRAGON PRESS
Whittier, California   1987

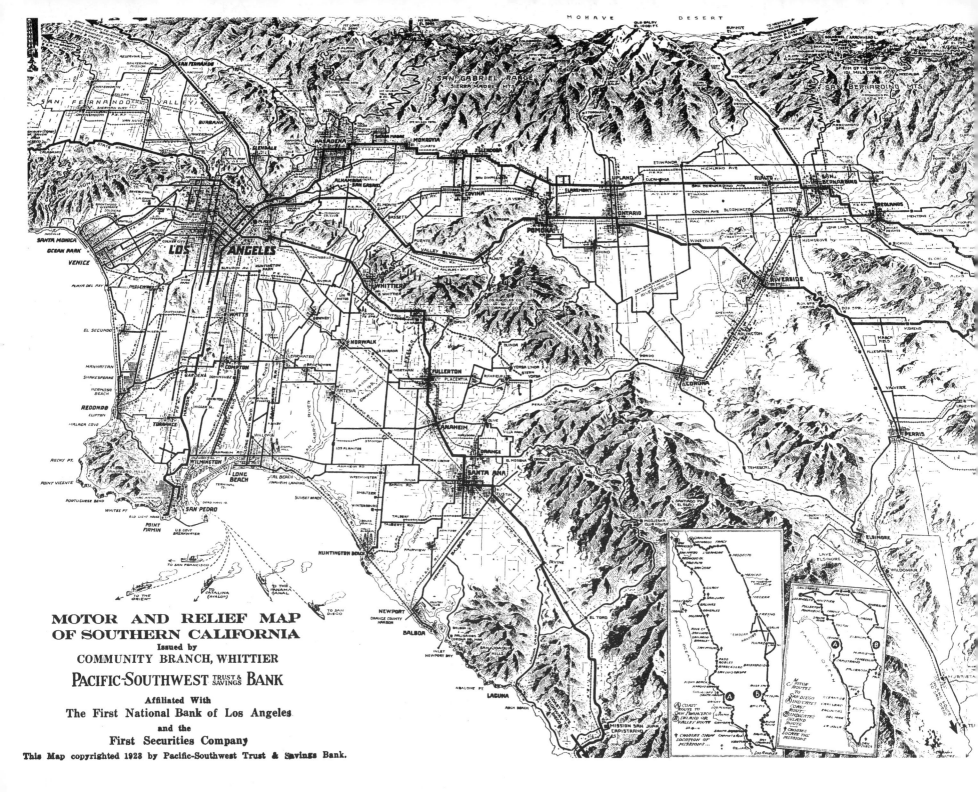

MOTOR AND RELIEF MAP
OF SOUTHERN CALIFORNIA

Issued by
COMMUNITY BRANCH, WHITTIER

PACIFIC-SOUTHWEST TRUST & SAVINGS BANK

Affiliated With
The First National Bank of Los Angeles
and the
First Securities Company

This Map copyrighted 1923 by Pacific-Southwest Trust & Savings Bank.

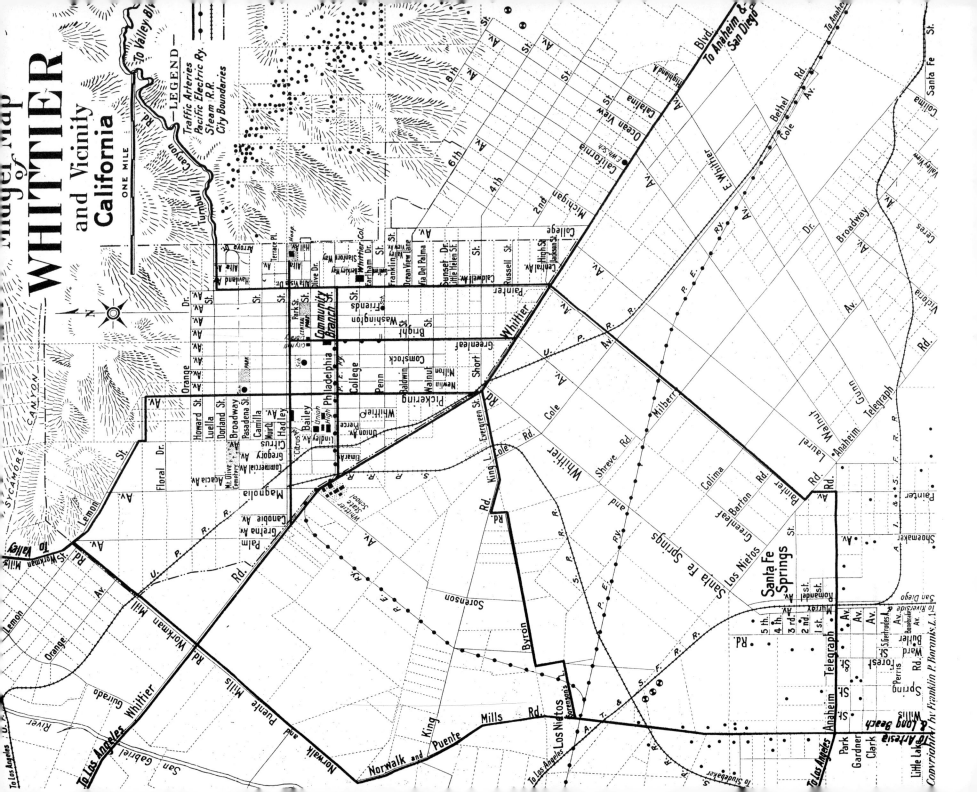

Intersection of Greenleaf and Hadley in 1893.

DEDICATED TO THE MEMORY OF
THE WHITTIER PIONEERS
WHOSE FAITH AND HARD WORK
MADE OUR CITY POSSIBLE.

This building, corner of Penn & Whittier Blvd. in 1903

ACKNOWLEDGEMENTS

A number of people have helped make this book a reality. They include Jack Hiddlestone whose book, *Greetings From Scranton*, gave me many good ideas on layout and design; Sam Guyan who gave a push in the right direction; Jim Barry and Lyle Nelson of the Bank of Whittier who had faith in this project; Kenny Ball, William Hockett, and Paul and Bob Gardner who contributed some of the card captions in the book; and Joe Da Rold, Executive Director of the Whittier Historical Society, without whose advice, support, and encouragement, this book would literally not have been possible. I am particularly indebted to Joe and to Bob Gardner for making available to me their Whittier postcards which served to round out my own collection. I am grateful also to many Whittier residents, too numerous to list, who contributed ideas, ancedotes, and postcards of early Whittier; to the Whittier Public Library and the Whittier Museum for making available valuable literary and graphic sources of information; and to the City of Whittier itself which, giving a warm welcome to me and my wife as newcomers, has encouraged us to make this lovely town our permanent home.

Back in 1933, a *History of Whittier* by Benjamin F. Arnold and Artilissa Dorland Clark was published that is a fascinating source of information about the early days of this city. To me it has served as an invaluable reference work. I recommend it highly to readers of this book who may want to know more about the beginnings of our community, especially about the far-sighted founders who built better than they knew. Other literary sources consulted are listed in the bibliography.

While many people have contributed material for this work, responsibility for any errors that have crept in is, of course, exclusively mine.

R.V.

Greenleaf Avenue looking north around 1920.

GREETINGS
FROM
WHITTIER

COPYRIGHT 1907
CUPPLES & LEON CO.
NEW YORK

CONTENTS

Greenleaf Avenue looking north around 1930.

INTRODUCTION

For those of us who have the privilege of living in Whittier in 1987, it is hard to believe that only one hundred years ago (when the parents of many of our current citizens were alive and thriving) the area of what is now "greater" Whittier was open farmland. Rising gently toward the northern hills, the clean-aired, sunny acres must have looked good to those few pioneer souls who had decided that this would be site of the first Quaker settlement in California. From the perspective of the beginning of the second century, we can look back on those first settlers with some envy. Apart from the pioneer spirit that thrives on being the first to break ground in a new land, they were blessed with fertile soil, potentially available water, a smog-free atmosphere, a slow-paced life, and (blessing of blessings!) a total absence of electronic devices.

They had to work hard, of course, but that was the norm. Where they could, they hired carpenters (at $4.00 a day); otherwise neighbor helped neighbor and with every available family member taking part, it was not long before houses and outbuildings began to go up. Small businesses and industry followed and suddenly a community had been established. Within a few short years of its founding in 1887, the town was ready to sit for its portrait. Enterprising postcard publishers discovered Whittier. For the next one hundred years, the change from a dusty village through the development of the truck farm, walnut, avocado, and citrus enterprises, to the establishment of a prosperous city was recorded on picture postcards.

The penny postcard (and they really *were* a penny!) was the mass communication medium of the time and they went all over the world. Southern California was a particularly popular subject. All the newly-transplanted Easterners could send postcards back in the middle of winter. Many of these cards showed fruit-laden orange groves with snow-capped mountains in the background, busy towns and cities, lovely green parks, beautiful schools and churches and public buildings . . . and the sunshine! Those cards were the Rose Parade telecasts of the time. How many thousands must have come to California lured as much by the postcard pictures as by the written message on the back!

Fortunately, many of those old postcards have been preserved (an entire industry is based on the collection of those bits of American history). Beautiful old Whittier churches, schools, homes, and public buildings that in the name of progress are long gone, still live in these colorful pieces of cardboard. Here and there among old Whittier cards can be seen homes and other buildings that have somehow managed to survive the mania for "development"–too few, sad to say, but they are still there.

There is a lesson here, it seems to me, for those who will guide Whittier in its second century. Perhaps we can learn from the destruction of the stately old library and the imposing Victorian houses, that a city's buildings are an integral part of its history and need to be protected. Somehow a balance must be found between the demands of progress and the preservation of our heritage.

This book is in part an attempt to preserve that heritage. From the postcards and other pictures included in this book, a history of the physical development of Whittier emerges. It is not complete, of course; I am sure that we do not have every postcard ever published of Whittier. Nor does this book do justice to the *people* who, after all, made everything happen. But there is enough here to get the *feel* for what the town must have been like in its beginnings and how it has changed over the years. With faith, hard work, and the ability to put to good use whatever resources were available, those early Friends (the Pickerings and the Baileys and the Hadleys; the Newlins and the Brights and the Lindleys) laid the foundations of what has become a community of which the entire state of California can be proud. A clean, well-governed city with exceptional police and public services, park and recreation facilities, commercial and industrial development, and pre-school to college education, Whittier has yet maintained that small-town friendliness that makes it simply a nice place to live.

I am proud and happy to be a part of the beginning of Whittier's second century and at the same time to pay tribute through this book to our predecessors who did so much for its first one hundred years.

Rudy Valdez
Whittier, CA
May, 1987

Vice-president Nixon and family in 1953.

UPTOWN

What is now the heart of "Uptown Whittier" was originally a tract consisting of 32 blocks of 5 acres each divided into town lots. Bounded on the west by Pickering Avenue, on the east by Painter, by Hadley on the north, and on the south by Penn, the area in the early part of 1887 quickly became the focus of building activity both residential and commercial. In that year a field of barley at the corner of Greenleaf and Philadelphia was harvested in order to permit the grading of the streets. By November a lumber yard had been established at Pickering and Philadelphia, a livery stable had opened at 110 North Milton, a small two-story building stood at the southwest corner of Greenleaf and Philadelphia, and the first house built in Whittier (except for the Bailey ranch house) stood at the corner of Milton and Philadelphia. On the opposite corner was a large boarding tent, the first "restaurant" in the city. Also constructed in that busy year were the Hotel Lindley at the southeast corner of Philadelphia and Bright (later moved to face Bright and re-named the Whittier Hotel), and the McStay Hotel at Penn and Greenleaf. At Hadley and Greenleaf four brick buildings were erected two of which still stand: the southwest corner building and the present Harvey apartments on the northeast corner. Meanwhile, in the "southern" part of town, other buildings were going up including the city's first bakery at the corner of Greenleaf and Penn.

The Packing House & Brick Yard around 1890.

Philadelphia st., Whittier, Cal.

This view, looking west on Philadelphia, appears to have been taken shortly after the completion of the Pacific Electric Railway lines in late 1903. - Joe Da Rold

A Part of the Business Section of Whittier, Cal.

Message: *"Dear Papa, Where I marked the cross [center] is where Uncle Charles is now but he intends to move as soon as they get a big building done where the bank is going to be."* [1906]

3

Business Street in Whittier, Cal.

Taken around 1905. Philadelphia Street looking west. Note the C.A. Rees Grocery and Western Union on the right.

Philadelphia Street, Whittier, Cal.

Looking east on Philadelphia. Whittier National Bank on left, First National Bank on right. Notice Pacific Electric tracks turning south on Greenleaf. [ca 1912] - William Hockett

Greenleaf Ave. looking South,
Whittier, Cal.

Greenleaf looking south. The building at the extreme left is the Masonic Temple currently occupied by the Knights of Columbus and Ames Bookstore on the ground floor. [1918]

The office of the Home Telephone Company was on the second floor of the building on the northwest corner of Bright and Philadelphia. Service began in 1904 with 80 telephones. Aubrey Wardman was the local manager - Joe Da Rold.

PHILADELPHIA STREET, LOOKING EAST.   WHITTIER, CAL.

5

Looking north on Greenleaf at the corner of Philadelphia. The Whittier National Bank Building on the right corner later became the United California Bank.

GREENLEAF AVENUE, WHITTIER, CALIFORNIA 0841

PHILADELPHIA ST. WHITTIER

Looking south on Philadelphia in the 30's. Note the clock on the Bank of America building on the left. - William Hockett.

Street Scene, Whittier, Calif. "Barton Studio" E3814

A similar view. The Bank of America building is where Richard Nixon had his first law office.

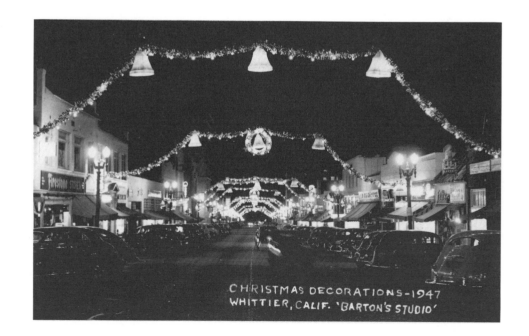

Christmas Decorations–1947 Whittier, Calif. 'Barton's Studio'

A night view of Greenleaf looking south, Christmas 1947. Whittier was famous for its uptown Christmas lights and decorations.

An early 1950's view of Greenleaf looking south. Compare this card with the one at the top of page 7.

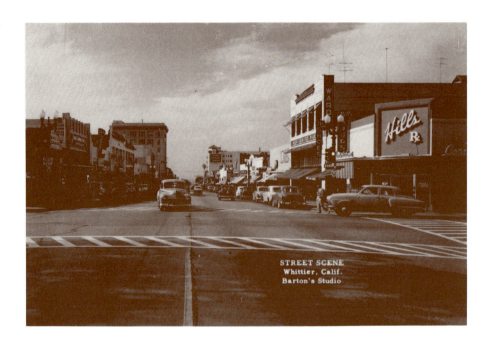

STREET SCENE
Whittier, Calif.
Barton's Studio

Street Scene   Whittier, Calif.

Northwest corner of Philadelphia and Greenleaf around 1952. The J.J. Newberry store was two doors up from the Owl drugstore.

Corner of Painter and Philadelphia around 1953. Jim Gerrard sold his market to Orcutt's who later sold to Bill Mifflin. Bentley's Drug Store was a favorite eating place for Whittier College students. The building burned down in 1970. - William Hockett.

Looking north on Greenleaf about 1953. Myer's Department Store was a well-known landmark and a favorite shopping place for Whittierites. - Joe Da Rold.

A similar view of Greenleaf around 1958.

Philadelphia looking east around 1950. The California Bank building was designed in 1932 in the "Art Deco" style by local architect William Harrison. Currently the "Crystal Room" restaurant on the second floor has retained the original decor. - Joe Da Rold.

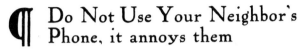
AROUND THE TOWN

A real estate boom that had swept Southern California (including Whittier) in 1887 collapsed in December of that year and the "depression" lasted until 1884. Nevertheless building continued, although at a much lower pace, and by 1895 Whittier boasted not only a business section but a considerable number of homes scattered throughout the settlement.

Over the years, Greenleaf, Painter, Washington, Friends, and other streets became important residential thoroughfares and many fine homes were built some of which are still standing. The addition of churches, schools, and more commercial buildings within 10 years of its founding gave Whittier the air of a well-established town.

As the city grew, it spread well beyond its original confines. Truck farms extending into East Whittier provided badly-needed income in the few years after the bust. A cannery established to process the San Gabriel tomato crop furnished employment to many Whittier residents who otherwise would have had no work at all. Then in 1893, work on the Whittier State School began that helped to bring the area out of the doldrums caused by the collapse of the real estate boom. By 1895 growth had begun in earnest and only 25 years later, Whittier could point to its residential areas, parks, schools, and churches as among the finest in the county.

Greenleaf looking south around 1930. Note the room rate on the Hoover Hotel.

Whittier from State School

Message: *"Dear Mama, in this picture shows where Maude is working & I will mark it* [center: white school building]. *My but it is a fine school house it is where we go to the entertainment or the lecture course. The state* [school] *is not very far from there and it's just grand. I haven't been all around it yet but I am going. Jennie.* [1907]

BIRDSEYE VIEW OF WHITTIER, CAL. LOOKING WEST ON PHILADELPHIA ST.

Taken around 1907. The building at the end of the street on the left is the State School.

Whittier, Cal.

Looking south from the hills. Whittier College is in the lower left hand corner. The high school is the white building at center right. Taken about 1907. - Paul Gardner

Residence Section, Whittier, Cal.

Taken around 1910. The Methodist church is at right center.

Philadelphia Street from the High School, Whittier, Cal.

The church in the lower right hand corner is the First Christian Church. Note the oil wells on the Puente Hills. Taken around 1910. - Paul Gardner

Orange Groves, Whittier, Cal.

In 1910 When this card was written there were many such groves in the Whittier area. A few trees from those stands are still in existence in the city.

This card is dated 1917.

North Washington Ave. Whittier, Cal.   632

Painter Avenue, Whittier, Cal.

Painter Avenue looking north from just below Philadelphia. The roof line at right center is the Mendenhall building at Whittier College. - William Hockett

16

A later view of Washington Avenue looking north from Broadway. The vehicle in the front is a delivery truck.

NORTH WASHINGTON AVENUE. WHITTIER, CALIFORNIA.

Also taken in 1925, the original clearly shows a "haze" in the distance. If it were not obviously spring or summer, the origin of the haze could have been citrus grower's smudge pots.

WHITTIER, CAL., LOOKING EAST.

17

BROADWAY. LOOKING SOUTH.   WHITTIER. CALIFORNIA

Taken about the same time as the cards on page 17. Despite the caption on the card, this is actually another view of Washington Avenue, this time looking south.

PALMS AND PEPPERS, PARK STREET WHITTIER, CAL.

Central, the city's first park, in on the right hand side of the picture. The pepper trees were eventually removed because they were too messy. - Paul Gardner

Woman's Club House, Whittier, Cal.

Located on the corner of Friends and Bailey, this building was used until around 1930 when a new structure was built on the same site. -Paul Gardner

In this air view of Whittier around 1925 it is possible to pick out some houses and other structures that are still in use in 1987.

WHITTIER, CAL., LOOKING SOUTH.

19

Northeast corner of Bailey and Friends. The house on the right is the home of A.C. Johnson who was president of the Whittier National Bank and a trustee of Whittier College. -William Hockett

Friends Ave. looking North, Whittier, Cal.

W-1   WOMAN'S CLUB, WHITTIER, CALIF

Erected in 1931 to replace the original wood frame structure, the building now houses the Rio Hondo Chapter of the American Red Cross. In the early 30's it was used by Whittier College for many social functions. - Kenny Ball

THE EAST WHITTIER UNITED PRESBYTERIAN CHURCH
1244 EAST SECOND STREET
WHITTIER, CALIFORNIA

HOUSES OF WORSHIP

The religious roots upon which Whittier was founded continue to play an important part in city life. Since that first meeting of the Friends in 1887 in the home of Jonathan Bailey, interest in the spiritual life has held steady with a wide variety of denominations represented in Whittier history. The Quakers, of course, were the founders of the town and their meeting house, built and donated by the Pickering Land and Water Company, was located at the corner of Comstock and College (not the present College Avenue). The second building erected in Whittier, it served the needs of the community of Friends for about ten years when the need for a new structure became evident.

Within two years of Whittier's founding, The First Methodist Episcopal Church was established. This was followed by the construction of the small Catholic Church of St. Mary's in 1893. In rapid succession, other faiths established their houses of worship: St. Mathias Episcopal Church in 1896; Christian Church, 1898; First Church of Christ Scientist in 1904; Federated Presbyterian, 1906; and the Church of Nazarene, 1907.

The Trinity Lutheran Church was founded in 1908; First Brethren in 1914, Calvary Baptist 1929, and the Church of Jesus Christ of Latter Day Saints in 1933. Since that time, other faiths have established houses of worship in the city.

Jonathan and Rebecca Bailey in front of their ranch house around 1890.
The first meetings of the Friends were held in this house in 1887.

Friends' Church, Whittier, Cal.

Taken around 1905, this shows the First Friends Church at the corner of Washington and Philadelphia. It was the first of three structures on this site.

A later view of the same church. [ca 1910]

Friend's Church, Whittier, Cal.

First Friend's Church, Whittier, California.

Erected in 1916 on the same site as the previous structure, this was the largest Friends Church in the world at the time. When enrollment rose at Whittier College after WWII, it was used for the college chapel and other meetings. - Kenny Ball

"The Little Brown Church" United (later *Federated*) Presbyterian Church. Built in 1911 and razed in 1952, it was located at the corner of College (now Wardman) and Bright.

Baptist Church, Whittier, Cal.

This first building was erected on the present church site at Bright and Bailey in 1889 at a cost of $2000. It was rebuilt in 1922. - Bob Gardner

The present Baptist Church at Bright and Bailey was dedicated in 1922.

First Baptist Church.

Located at Greenleaf and Hadley. Taken around 1932.

This is actually *Plymouth* Congregational. It stood at the corner of Wardman and Bright on the site now occupied by Lutheran Towers. [ca 1914]

Methodist Church, Whittier, Cal.

Located at the corner of Friends and Bailey. The Methodist Episcopal Church was erected in 1904 and replaced by the present church in 1952.

First Catholic services in Whittier were offered by a priest who came over from Mission San Gabriel or the Cathedral in Los Angeles. The church pictured here was dedicated in 1893. It was located at Newlin and Wardman. [ca 1929] - Bob Gardner

St. Mary's Catholic Church   Whittier, Calif.

Second building used by the Presbyterian Church in Whittier. The first was dedicated in 1911.

First Presbyterian Church   Whittier, California

St. Bruno's church in East Whittier, built in 1955, was one of five Catholic parishes established by the late Cardinal McIntyre.

WHITTIER COLLEGE

Whittier

By Mrs. Ella C. Veeder
Whittier, Cal.

The city of Whittier, California, was named in honor of John G. Whittier the Quaker poet.

Where Whittier stands, once the mus-
    tard bloom
Over-spread the ground, like the woof in a
    loom,
Shimmered and glowed in the sunshine warm,
Like the gold lace on a uniform.

Multitudes came, as effect follows
    cause,
Demonstrating the fact that mustard draws.
All went to work as busy as bees,
Building and plowing and planting trees.

Now the fruits mature, and the flowers
    grow faster,
Where Whittier wore the mustard plaster.
High School, and College and works of art,
Prove that the mustard made Whittier smart.

Friends, come to Whittier, and come to
    stay,
Where the golden mustard once held sway.

SMITH, WHITTIER   COPYRIGHT APPLIED FOR

The idea of a Quaker Academy in Whittier is almost as old as the city itself. Within a year of the founding, a college board had already been selected (headed by Dr. Samuel Coffin) and early in 1888 the town leaders eagerly pledged the money necessary for a million bricks (to be made in Whittier) and to hire an architect to work on plans for a college building to cost some $100,000. Unhappily it was just at that time the land boom collapse was under way and the vision, for the moment at least, soon vanished.

But not the idea. Despite the financial setbacks, an academy actually began in 1891 in what was then the new Reynolds building on East Philadelphia. This bare-bones Friends school was the start of what was eventually to become Whittier College but it began as a grade school. (It was not until much later that the *college* came into being.) With Dr. Coffin leading the effort, a site was secured, funds raised, and by 1893 work had actually begun on what was to become Founders Hall. This despite the fact that not even half the money required to complete the project was yet in hand. Here again, apparently inexhaustable faith sustained the community. With volunteer as well as paid help the site was cleared and graded, the foundation laid and actual construction started. With the second story not yet finished, the first class of fifty students and four teachers began in the new building on March 28, 1894.

But it was still merely an academy. Ten years of poverty, struggle, doubts, and setbacks were to go by before the actions of the indomitable Friends in sustaining and supporting the institution were to secure a charter for Whittier *College*. With that, however, the slow but steady growth of the institution into a position of great influence in the community began. Friends throughout the country started a plan of support that has never really ended and almost one hundred years after its beginning, Whittier College is secure in its niche as a unique and highly successful institution of higher education.

13111 E. Philadelphia St., built in 1888, birthplace
of Whittier College, torn down in 1967

Whittier College, Whittier, Cal.

A new building for the 51 students enrolled in 1894. Founder's Hall was destroyed by fire on Friday, December 13, 1968. - William Hockett

Whittier College, Whittier, Cal.

My father, Howard L. Hockett, came to Whittier in 1914 as head of the music department at Whittier College. In 1933 he became comptroller and remained in that position until he died in 1954. His first studio was the room in the upper right of the building. - William Hockett

31

WHITTIER COLLEGE - WHITTIER, CAL.

Message: *"Whittier, August 19, 1923. Dear Jer, I am visiting the Porrs...This is a wonderfully rich city. It was founded by Quakers...About a mile from here at Santa Fe Springs are hundreds of oil wells...the State Reform School is located here. Your sister, Joe"*

WHITTIER COLLEGE. WHITTIER, CAL.

Taken around 1925

32

This was the main building at Whittier College until it burned down. Most of the rooms were typical classrooms. The basement housed science classes with lab facilities. The assembly room was used for chapel, plays, assemblies, etc. The seating capacity was about 400. I attended Whittier College from 1930 to 1935. - Kenny Ball

Originally Founders' Hall was a red brick building. In the mid-1930's it was plastered as the picture below [ca 1965] indicates. - Kenny Ball

One of the last pictures taken of old Founders Hall.

WARDMAN HALL and GYM
WHITTIER COLLEGE, WHITTIER, CALIF.   C 334

Wardman Hall has been both a men's and women's dormitory since the 1920's. Wardman gym on the right was the athletic center until the new Don Graham Activities Center was completed. - Kenny Ball

Platner Hall has served as a women's dormitory from the 1920's to date. - Kenny Ball

PLATNER HALL, WHITTIER COLLEGE, WHITTIER, CALIF.

1452:—Wardman Hall, Whittier College, Whittier, Calif.

Sometime around 1929, Aubrey Wardman made a gift to Whittier College of $200,000 (then said to represent two weeks' income from his oil wells in Santa Fe Springs). The money was used to build the dorm and Wardman gym.
 William Hockett

The Mendenhall Administration Building was the former Elks Lodge. It was acquired by the college in the 1930's. It also served as the library until the Bonnie Wardman building was completed. - Kenny Ball

Another view of the administration building taken around 1955.

WHITTIER STATE SCHOOL
(JOHN C. NELLES)

It is somewhat ironic that a church-founded city would have to depend on the state's penal system for its economic salvation but to a considerable extent that is what happened shortly after Whittier was established. With the collapse of the land boom in 1887-1889, the population of the town had been reduced from a high of one thousand to something closer to four hundred. Times were hard; work was scarce. Many people had left or were thinking about leaving because there appeared to be no future in the town. But again a driving force came forward. Convinced that a juvenile facility was badly needed and that its local construction would provide sorely-needed relief, Hervey Lindley of Los Angeles led the campaign that was to result in the establishment of the state school in Whittier. He secured the donation of 40 acres for the school and lobbied for the necessary legislation in Sacramento that set up the "State Reform School for Juvenile Offenders." Lindley, James R. Lowe from San Jose, and Nevada City's Josia Sims became the institutions founding trustees. One of their first acts was to select Walter Lindley of Los Angeles as superintendent of the school.

On February 12, 1890, a large gathering on the site (that included the governor of California) witnessed the laying of the cornerstone. Taking first things first however, the board had the grounds laid out and landscaped, built a barn with cowsheds, a corral, poultry buildings, and finally the administration building itself: an imposing structure with four stories and a basement with a central tower overlooking the entire complex.

How the youngsters fared here, then and now, is another story but in those first years, at least, every boy and girl was expected to learn a trade that could earn them a living. Among other things the boys could learn carpentry, painting, printing, animal husbandry and dairying, tailoring and shoemaking. The girls were trained in homemaking skills including dressmaking. Because of the work done by the boys and girls, the facility was virtually self-sufficient.

I remember seeing the cadets marched up Philadelphia to see the movies at the *Scenic* (lately the *Roxy*) theatre. This would have been in the 20's or 30's. - William Hockett

WOOD'S PRINT, L. A. State Reform School, Whittier, California

This card has an undivided back which means it was printed prior to 1907 when the first divided-back cards were issued. Note also the name which was later changed as noted below.

State School, Whittier, Cal.

In 1883, Hervey Lindley petitioned the governor to change the name from "Reform School for Juvenile Offenders" to "Whittier School of Trades and Agriculture." After Superintendent Fred C. Nelles's death in 1927, the school was given its present name. [ca 1913] - Joe Da Rold

In the early days, the boy residents were called "cadets" and were organized into battalions. They took part in daily activities based on military formation and drills.

Taken around 1908, this scene shows the school's military band which was used throughout the area in many public parades.

State School for Boys, Whittier, Cal.   636

Message: *My dear Mrs. Smith, I am having such a good time in East Whittier have been here just a week may stay another...It is very pleasant here, such beautiful sunrises and sunsets. I walked to Whittier to church and back (about 4 miles) yesterday a.m. Love to all Mary E. Green. [ca 1910]*

Maintenance of the school was the responsibility of the cadets. As this scene taken around 1910 indicates, they took pride in the beautiful grounds.

Park Scene in the grounds of the Whittier State School, Whittier, Cal.

State School, Girl's Department, Whittier, Cal.

This was taken prior to 1914 when a separate department for girls was established and moved to Ventura in January of that year. -Joe Da Rold

STATE SCHOOL, WHITTIER, CALIFORNIA CH203

Many of the Whittier College men students worked at the state school (mostly as dorm resident supervisors) sleeping in the quarters with the boys at night during the 1930's. I delivered milk to the school for the Whittier Sanitary Dairy from 1933 to 1936. - Kenny Ball

SCHOOLS AND SCHOOL CHILDREN

Although the first school in the Whittier area was opened as early as 1883 (a little 10′ x 12′ structure for some dozen youngsters), it was not until 1885 that the Evergreen school was built on what is now Painter Avenue just north of the present Whittier Boulevard. This facility antedated the founding of the town by two years. With constantly-growing attendance another school became necessary and Bailey Street (between Comstock and Milton) was opened in 1889. These two sites served the needs of the area until 1900 when it became apparent that a high school was needed. Accordingly the Bailey Street site became the high school and a building at the corner of Greenleaf and Hadley (one of the original four bricks) was rented for the elementary grades. Enrollment grew at such a pace that by 1897 the third and fourth grades each contained as many as 60 or 70 pupils and there were 75 to 80 youngsters in grades one and two. To reduce the pressure, a new school was built at the corner of Penn and Washington in 1902 and ten years later Pickering and Broadway became the site of still another elementary facility. In 1915, the John Greenleaf Whittier School was built followed by Longfellow, Lydia Jackson, and the new Jonathan Bailey school all built in 1926. In the meantime surrounding school districts had also been busy. East Whittier had built their school in 1903; Santa Gertrudes (now South Whittier) in 1911; and Los Nietos in 1908.

The forming of the Whittier Union High School District in 1903 led to bond issues that made possible the construction of the first high school building in 1905. This was followed by a science hall and manual arts building and a gymnasium all completed by 1912.

South Whittier Intermediate School--South Whittier

Baily Street School, Whittier, Cal.

I attended the old Bailey School in 1923 and 1924. My fifth and sixth grade teachers were Miss Anna May Moody and Miss Shoemaker. -William Hockett

PENN ST. GRAMMAR SCHOOL, WHITTIER, CAL.

I went to Penn Street School from 1918 to 1922. We were marched to the classroom to the beat of a triangle. The school stood at the site of the present Whittier Square. - William Hockett

45

E.K. Bishop was principal of John Muir School for the entire period of its existence. At the time it was the only school where 7th and 8th grades were taught. - William Hockett

1423:—John Muir School, Whittier, Calif.

"On the Coast Highway"

Broadway Grammar School, Whittier, Cal.

The Broadway Grammer School occupied a site at the corner of Broadway and Pickering.

WHITTIER AVENUE SCHOOL, WHITTIER, CALIFORNIA.

Present site of the Whittier School District administration headquarters. The playground is supervised by the city recreation department and gets lots of summer use. - Kenny Ball

The Lydia Jackson School, built in 1926, is still in use.

Message: *"Whittier, July 13, 1916. My dear Ella, I suppose that you will be surprised to learn that we are living here now...We live just back of Owen at 126 S. Whittier Ave. Love ...Rose H."*

Grades three and four at East Whittier School in 1911. Note the elaborate bows on some of the girls.

This would appear to be an upper elementary grade, perhaps a 5/6 combination class. Taken at East Whittier School in 1910.

The fairly well-matched size of the girls and the variations in size of boys would indicate that this 1912 East Whittier group is probably an 8th grade.

49

Much of this building was destroyed in an earthquake. It was rebuilt and is in use today. -Kenny Ball

Los Nietos school. Taken around 1960.

UNION HIGH SCHOOL, WHITTIER, CAL.

Original building of the Whittier Union High School. Badly damaged in the 1933 earthquake, it was later demolished. - William Hockett

High School, Whittier, Cal.

A view of the old high school in 1914. Note the additions.

A still later view around 1918. Note the hats on the men and the girls in black stockings.

Message: [Written to New Jersey in February, 1922] *"Dear Sister, I see by the papers you folks have lots of cold weather and lots of snow... We have no snow but the weather is anything but warm. Frost every morning 42 above... have to have a fire mostly all day..."*

The auditorium of President Nixon's high school. This is the last one built. The preceding one was badly damaged in the 1933 earthquake and after standing idle for many years was rebuilt as the library. - William Hockett

HIGH SCHOOL AUDITORIUM
WHITTIER, CALIF. "BARTON STUDIO" E3802

Monte Vista School, South Whittier School District. Taken in 1953.

The library and mall of Rio Hondo College as viewed from the science building. Taken around 1960.

Former site of the Lowell Joint School District's Lowell High School, it became the new campus of the Los Angeles College of Chiropractic in 1981.

HOTELS

HOTEL HOOVER
WHITTIER, CALIFORNIA

13 Miles SE of Downtown
Los Angeles on HIWAY 101

The energetic efforts of the Pickering Land and Water Company to promote the sale of its lots led to a large migration of people into the area. The first comers often stayed in nearby settlements such as Norwalk or Santa Fe Springs or else (like the Dorland family), pitched tents right on their land; the need for public accommodations became obvious. By 1887, Whittier's first hotel, the Whittier, had been built. A modest frame structure, it was followed shortly by C.W. Harvey's hotel, a more elaborate and comfortable building that was later moved and re-named the Greenleaf. These early hostelries provided the necessary accommodations until comparatively recent times when more modern hotels were built.

Arnold lists six Whittier hotels in 1932. At that time they were fairly new and probably included both permanent and transient residents. They served the needs not only of Whittier itself but the surrounding areas as well. First on Arnold's list was the Continental built in 1924. Today it serves as a transient hotel for low-income people and on the ground floor houses the Valdez Bookstore. Also listed and currently used as rooming houses or low-priced hotels are the Greenleaf and the Hoover on Greenleaf and the Bright and Whittier Hotels on Bright Avenue.

The William Penn, Whittier's finest hostelry, was for many years the center of much of the city's social and civic activities. Here, many of the service and fraternal organizations as well as city agencies held their regular meetings and social functions. Badly damaged in a fire in 1979, the William Penn structure survived for several years while its fate was debated by the city. It was finally demolished in 1985. The opening of the handsome new Hilton Hotel on Greenleaf in 1986 has, to the delight of the city, replaced the ameneties formerly provided by the William Penn.

The New Hilton Hotel on Greenleaf. Inaugurated in 1986.

Taken around 1890. The Whittier Hotel stood at the corner of Bright and Philadelphia.

C.W. Harvey's hotel was built in 1887 on Painter between Broadway and Beverly. It was later moved to the southwest corner of Greenleaf and Bailey and renamed the Greenleaf. [ca 1905] - Paul Gardner

57

Hotel Greenleaf, Whittier, Cal.

My family stayed in this hotel for a week in 1917 waiting for a house to be completed. It was run by a family named Pickett. - William Hockett

Built in 1924, the William Penn Hotel was the one time great hotel of Whittier until it was destroyed by fire in 1978. Many well-known people stayed there. It was the meeting place for many civic organizations and it housed the Chamber of Commerce and several businesses. - Kenny Ball

COMMERCIAL

The commercial aspects of life in Whittier have occupied the attention of its citizens from the very beginning. Recognizing that a permanent settlement would require many services and commodities, enterprising residents soon began to provide for such demands.

First of all, of course, was the need to acquire, sub-divide, and sell land and the Pickering Land and Water Company was formed in 1887 for just this purpose. The Thomas and Turnbull ranches became their stock in trade and land sales were brisk until the end of 1887 when the land boom broke. Soon, however, truck gardens sprang up in the area the produce of which was then hauled to Los Angeles and sold to bring in badly-needed income to the city.

Walter Vernon's lumber yard at Pickering and Philadelphia opened in 1887 and by 1890 a cannery on West Philadelphia and brick yard on West Hadley were helping the town to recover from the recession. In those days every town needed a livery stable and as early as 1888 one had been opened at 110 North Milton. J. H. Gwin, the owner of the stable, later opened a grocery store across the street that, after being moved to a new location on Philadelphia, stayed in business well into the twenties. By July of 1887 a public eating place (housed in a tent) had opened at the corner of Philadelphia and Milton. Before the collapse of the land fever, the town included a bakery, a drugstore, a general merchandise store and post office at the corner of Greenleaf and Philadelphia, and even a newspaper (*The Graphic*) in the Masonic Temple site.

Eventually, Whittier became the most important commercial center of the entire area. By the 1920's virtually everything that a city dweller or a farmer needed could be purchased in Whittier. In the uptown area particularly, local business competed with national chains such as the Golden Rule Store (later J.C. Penney's), Montgomery Ward, Kress, and others. The professional services of doctors, lawyers, and dentists had been available almost from the very beginning.

A popular department store on north Greenleaf in 1910.

An early motorcycle shop (Stanfield's) in uptown Whittier around 1910. (No, that is not Mark Twain on the motorcycle.)

1450A:—Philadelphia Street, Whittier, Calif.

Philadelphia Street business area in the mid 20's. Ginston's shoe store seems to be flying the flag.

The Whittier Savings Bank was at the north-east corner of Greenleaf and Philadelphia. (See card below)

Looking north on Greenleaf at Philadelphia around 1940.

New Home of
Whittier Sanitary Dairy Co.
126-138 S. Comstock Ave., Whittier, California
VISITORS ARE ALWAYS WELCOME
Plant in full operation daily — 9 A.M. to 3 P.M.

The Whittier Sanitary Dairy (later named Quaker Maid) was operated by the Lautrop and Ball families from 1923 until 1981 when it was sold to Carnation. The building shown was built in 1949, one of the most modern plants in Southern California. Part of it is still standing.
- Kenny Ball

John Ball, son of Kenny Ball and grandson of L.C. Lautrop, making a home delivery in 1960.
-Kenny Ball

1451A:—Murphy Memorial Hospital, Whittier, Calif.

I served on the special board that operated Murphy Hospital until it was closed in 1965. The property was later sold to Whittier College and used as a dorm and storage site. It was demolished in 1985 and is now the site of Murphy Hill condominiums. - Kenny Ball

THEY COME FROM ALL DIRECTIONS, 50 MILES AND MORE DAILY—90% FAMILY TRADE.

NO BOOZE—NO JAZZ—JUST GOOD HOME COOKED FOODS.

WE SERVE ABOUT 10,000 CUSTOMERS PER MONTH.

Holland Inn

HOLLAND INN, 716 EAST WHITTIER BLVD. (U. S. HIGHWAY 101) WHITTIER. CALIF.

VISIT OUR KITCHEN—ALL WOMEN EMPLOYEES—100% STATE HEALTH EXAMINATIONS.

Holland Inn was a fine family restaurant serving home-cooked type meals. People would come from miles around. It is now the site of the Elks Lodge. - William Hockett

Myers, established in 1905 was a fine, locally-owned department store. It was eventually sold to the Boston Stores chain. The Myers family has contributed much to Whittier's civic affairs. - Kenny Ball

This large drive-in was owned by Don Nixon the president's brother and managed by Bill Milhouse, his first cousin. It was a favorite of teen-agers in particular. - Kenny Ball

The Whittier Quad in its heyday in the 60's. At the time it was one of the largest and finest shopping centers in the southland.

When I went to high school in 1929-30, this was the most popular movie house. The outstanding feature was the ceiling full of lighted stars and fleecy clouds. - Kenny Ball

The theater was built outside the city limits so films could be shown on Sundays. At first, talent shows and Vaudeville were shown along with the films. - Paul Gardner

PUBLIC BUILDINGS

There is some uncertainty as to the location of the city's *first* municipal offices but there is one building still standing that served at one time as an early city hall, court house, and council chambers, and police station. Pictured on page 69, this civic center was located on Comstock just north of Wardman. One of the buildings later became part of the Quaker Dairy complex and was spared when in 1987, a section of the dairy building was demolished.

This book uses the term "public building" rather broadly; some of the structures pictured in this section are privately owned. They are included, however because of their use in a variety of ways by the community. Examples of this are the Women's Club, the Masonic Temple, and the YMCA.

The heavy emphasis placed on the old library in this section is deliberate. An almost perfect example of the kinds of structures built with the help of Andrew Carnegie, the library had a beauty, a dignity, an atmosphere, and even a delightfully bookish smell, that no new structure can match. This is not intended to denigrate in any was the present facility which is highly functional and efficient and the staff of which serves the community better than ever. But that old building can never be replaced. The only thing we have now is the pictures and they are really just a pale approximation of the real thing. To those who knew the old library it was a place to go of an afternoon or evening, peaceful and quiet, with the old oak shelves and fixtures a part of its presence and beauty. A place to hear stories read or to discover for one' self the joys of *Tom Sawyer* and *David Copperfield*, of Emily Dickenson and Alexander Dumas.

The new city hall on Penn is still new. It, too, has a unique beauty. Let's hope that fifty or sixty years from today it is recognized as a building worth saving and that the pressure of progress does not make it suffer the same fate as the old library.

Presbyterian Intercommunity Hospital.
Kenny Ball served on its board for 27 years beginning when it was the Murphy Hospital.

Whittier City Hall around 1950. The city court was located on the second floor above the police department. It also served as the city council chambers. - William Hockett

The City Hall in the 80's. Designed by local architect William H. Harrison, the new facility opened in 1955. It was the first municipal building erected since 1923. - Joe Da Rold

Public Library, Whittier, Cal.

The Whittier WCTU organized a public reading room in 1888. By 1903, the average daily circulation was 34 books. [1908] - Joe Da Rold

Public Library, Whittier, Cal.

The Whittier Public Library opened in 1907. Andrew Carnegie donated $14,500. The site at Bailey and Greenleaf was obtained for $7000. Construction cost $9948. - Joe Da Rold

When the old library building was demolished in the late 50's, the 8-foot high front door shown here was salvaged by Dr. Max Flanders. It is now the door to the archives room of the Whittier Museum. - Joe Da Rold

The lovely old library as it looked in the early forties. Compare the foliage to the picture on page 70.

One of the last pictures taken of the old library. What fun we had going down to listen to the evening story hour dressed in our pajamas. - Bob Gardner

The Women's Club at Bailey and Friends. It is now the headquarters of the Rio Hondo Chapter of the American Red Cross.

WHITTIER WOMAN'S CLUB - 1935

The post-office was constructed in the mid-thirties at the height of the depression through a Public Works Administration grant. Like the other post-offices built throughout the country at the same time, it was designed to withstand ten feet of snow. - William Hockett

The YMCA building [which is still in use] was completed in 1948. When the facility was new it was used as a meeting place by the Lions Club while the William Penn Hotel dining room was being remodeled. - William Hockett

The Whittier Art Gallery--still currently in use--was built on land donated by Fred Pease at Painter and Mooreland. - Paul Gardner

The Whittier Masonic Lodge at the corner of Greenleaf and Mar Vista in the 70's.

PARKS

Like schools, parks were an early priority for the Whittier founders. The original layout of the city included space for Central Park which was first developed in 1887 and redeveloped in 1982. As the area has grown the city fathers have continued to provide these important amenities throughout the community. By 1910, the need for additional facilities was recognized and the Broadway setting was developed from 1912 to 1920. In 1939, the Beverly Fountain (later renamed the Lou Henry Hoover) was installed and about the same time (from 1938 to 1942) Penn Park, Friends, and York came into the system. Between 1944 and 1950, Palm and Laurel became available for public use and from 1965 to 1967, Michigan and Parnell Parks were developed.

By 1968 the original cemetaries of Whittier on Citrus Avenue, dating back to the turn of the century, had become a blight on the area because of long neglect. The city reclaimed the land, installed walks, benches, and a few picnic tables and landscaped with flowering shrubs and trees. This became Founders Park which was dedicated as a memorial to those who had found there a final resting place.

In 1969, Leffingwell (which includes four tennis courts and is lighted for night use) and Murphy Ranch (developed as a natural park with riding and hiking trails) were brought into the group. John Greenleaf Whittier (a neighborhood playground) came into use in 1976, Guirado Park on Pioneer Boulevard in 1979, and Anaconda (also a neighborhood park) have completed the system to date. An additional 200 acres in the Hellman estate are in reserve for future development as a wilderness park.

A visitor to any of Whittier's parks can easily detect the pride taken by the groundskeepers in maintaining the beauty of these areas so essential to the well-being of the city.

E148 Eucalyptus Trees Lower Campus Whittier College Calif.

Central Park around 1910. Shown are the children of the Reverend William Stevens. The lady is Helen Cooper.

City Park, Whittier, Cal.   635

Another view of Central Park also in the early 1900's. The old band shell was located where the restrooms are today. - William Hockett

An early park scene. Note the horse-drawn wagon on the right.

Park Scene in Whittier, Cal.

Park at Whittier, Cal.

Presumed to have been taken around 1900 so it probably shows Central Park.

Scene at Central Park, Whittier, Cal.

1603

Message: "*401 S. Painter Ave., Dear Josephine, Of course you know I am here in California...It is a beautiful country of sunshine and flowers. Have seen frost twice and only snow on the mountain tops. The roses, geraniums, and all the flowers and oranges on the trees make it seem unlike midwinter. Love, Mary Ballar.*"

A VIEW IN THE PARK
WHITTIER · CAL.
5061

Central Park. In May of 1910, the city council decided to pay band members the sum of $1.00 each to play in the park band shell but the total was not to exceed $15.00. - Bob Gardner

79

This fountain has been renamed for Lou Henry Hoover, the wife of President Hoover. -Kenny Ball

Beverly Fountain   Whittier Calif.

This is a view in Penn Park. It was built by the WPA in the 40's. Part of the land for the park was donated by Vic York. - Kenny Ball

THE PICO MANSION

The Pico House in 1932.

In 1826, following his wedding in Los Angeles, Don Pio Pico and his bride rode east to what is now the area of Whittier. Here they decided to build their home which was eventually to consist of thirty-three rooms surrounding a central "patio" or courtyard. Beautifully landscaped, furnished at tremendous expense, and decorated with the opulent taste of the period, the mansion became the center of social life and political action in the southland. Don Pio became famous for his hospitality and, far from the center of power in Mexico City, he wielded an influence that was to result in his becoming governor of California on two different occasions, the last of which came at the time of the American conquest of the province.

After California became a state Pico continued to live in his mansion but little by little through chicanery and trickery he was despoiled of his lands and he died in poverty in 1894.

Meanwhile, wasted by a disastrous flood and almost total neglect, the once magnificent house was reduced to a few crumbling adobe structures. In 1898, six acres of the Pico ranch were purchased by the city of Whittier for the sinking of water wells and in 1902 a movement was started to restore the old landmark. Organized as the Pio Pico Historical Society, a group of women from East Whittier and Whittier were instrumental in putting at least a temporary halt to the ravages suffered by the structure. Eventually, the site became a state historical monument and with additional restoration work, the mansion is now maintained as a museum which is open to the public at its site near the intersection of Pioneer and Whittier Boulevards.

Readers wishing to know more about this fascinating man and his home are referred to the Martin Cole work listed in the bibliography.

Don Pio Pico's Mansion, Last Spanish Governor of California, Near Whittier, Cal.

Actually, Pio Pico was the last *Mexican* governor of California.

A view of the Pico mansion taken around 1910.

Interior patio of the Pico home also taken around 1910.

A view of the mansion prior to its restoration.

Old Home of Don Pio Pico, near Whittier, Cal.

Legend has it that Don Pio and his bride stopped for the noon-day meal on their wedding day and chose the spot for their new home. - Bob Gardner

A MISCELLANY

RICHARD MILHOUS NIXON
President of the United States

Whittier in one hundred years has, perhaps more than any of its neighbors, managed to maintain its community identity. Anchored as it were by the original uptown plat, the city despite its growth, held firmly to much of its founders' philosophy of conservatism in virtually all aspects of city life. It is this close link with the past that has enabled the city to resist many of the evils of urbanization.

While this section begins with a portrait of its most famous son, (who, politically at least, embodies that Quaker conservatism) it reverts to the past in the pictures that follow to emphasize the roots of the community and the celebration of one hundred years of growth.

It must be left to others to record for the bicentennial one hundred years hence what Whittier is like today. Inevitably, change will come. Already, the long-anticipated extension of Hadley through the hills to Hacienda Heights appears to be getting closer to reality. The redevelopment centered on the core city will change drastically the appearance of the southern and western edges of "Uptown" Whittier. The demographic changes already obvious will accelerate and impose new ideas on what the city will look like. Will it continue to be a city of homes—or will development bring more apartments and condominiums to the city? Will the Puente Hills survive the inevitable population pressures? Will freeway extensions double and triple our population? Only our grandchildren will know the answers—they too, in 2087, will be celebrating the event that, in 1887, made the existence of this lovely city possible.

Richard M. Nixon, Whittier's most famous citizen, was inaugurated President of the United States on January 20, 1969. A graduate of Whittier High and Whittier College, Mr. Nixon served as congressman and senator from California from 1952 to 1956 and as vice president from 1961 to 1963.

The Dashwood House. Home of president Nixon's maternal grandparents.

A crew of walnut pickers on the latest high-wheeled International truck.

Morgan Morago's stockyard at Whittier Avenue and Philadelphia. The horse-drawn wagon is carrying fumigating equipment. [1914] - Joe Da Rold

The "Four Bricks" minus one. Corner of Greenleaf and Hadley. [ca 1887]

Turnbull Canyon Boulevard, between Whittier & Pomona, Whittier, Cal.

This road was improved by mostly "hand-work" under WPA program in the 1930's. Kenny Ball

Oil Fields, Whittier, California.

Oil derricks proliferated from Montebello to La Habra but Whittier's city council wisely passed an ordinance in the early 1920's that prohibited drilling within the city limits. Nevertheless the booming oil industry brought many new residents to Whittier. - Joe Da Rold

Air view of the Kruse Dairy in what was then the Pico area. It was operated mostly as a cash and carry retail dairy. Walter Kruse died recently. He was a highly-regarded citizen of the area. The dairy is still in operation. - Kenny Ball

The Pacific Electric line to Whittier was started in 1903. They operated between Los Angeles and Whittier until 1938. Many Whittier College students rode these cars to school from the Huntington Park, Maywood, Bell and Rivera areas during the 1920's. - Joe Da Rold and Kenny Ball

PACIFIC ELECTRIC NO. 257
TYPICAL EARLY "CALIFORNIA-TYPE" INTERURBAN

WHITTIER, CALIF.
1908

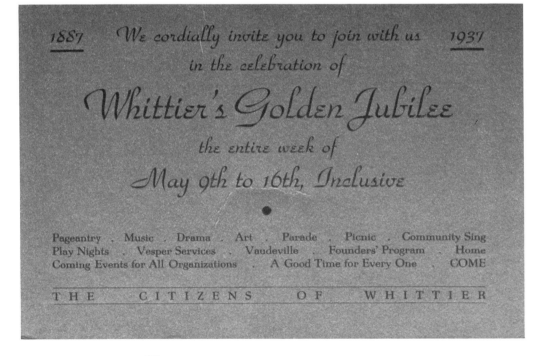

1887   We cordially invite you to join with us   1937
in the celebration of

Whittier's Golden Jubilee

the entire week of

May 9th to 16th, Inclusive

•

Pageantry . Music . Drama . Art . Parade . Picnic . Community Sing
Play Nights . Vesper Services . Vaudeville . Founders' Program . Home
Coming Events for All Organizations . A Good Time for Every One . COME

THE   CITIZENS   OF   WHITTIER

Whittier's Golden Jubilee was celebrated proudly for one "entire week." In 1987 the Whittier Centennial lasted five months culminating on Founders' Day in May. - Joe Da Rold

Greenleaf Avenue looking north. [ca 1900]

S. E. corner of Philadelphia & Greenleaf in the 90's

Photo-copy by Espolt

BIBLIOGRAPHY

Chapel: Rose Hills Memorial Park

Arnold, Benjamin F. and Artilissa Dorland Clark.
HISTORY OF WHITTIER, Whittier, CA Western Printing Corp.,
1933, 395 pp.

Carler, Coila, HISTORY OF WHITTIER: A Thesis Presented in
Partial Fulfillment of the Degree for AB at Whittier College
Department of History, Whittier College, 1908, 21 pp.

Cole, Martin, PIO PICO MISCELLANY, Whittier, CA, Governor Pico
Mansion Society, 1978, 106 pp, illust.

Crosfield, Gulielma, TWO SUNNY WINTERS IN CALIFORNIA,
London, Headley, 1904, 187 pp, illust.

Mohler, Ruth Ann, PIONEER DAYS OF WHITTIER, Whittier,
CA, 1927, 14 pp.

Pearce, Phyllis M. et. al., FOUNDERS AND FRIENDS, Whittier, CA
Rio Hondo College Community Services, 1977, viii, 125 pp, photos.

RECALLING PIONEER DAYS, WHITTIER: 50th BIRTHDAY
CELEBRATION, 1937, Newspaper clippings prepared by Writers'
Section, American Association of University Women, Whittier
Branch, as their contribution to the success of the 50th birthday
celebration. May 9-11, 1937

Sharpless, Caroline Rebessa, HISTORY OF WHITTIER AS REGARDS
THE QUAKERS, Whittier College, 1910, 18 pp.

Whittier News, FIFTIETH ANNIVERSARY EDITION, May 11, 1937.

Zimmer, Florence, WHITTIER, LONG AGO AND TODAY, illustrated
by Bob Gardner, Whittier, CA, 1984.

PICTURE CREDITS

PAGE	SOURCE	PUBLISHER	PAGE	SOURCE	PUBLISHER	PAGE	SOURCE	PUBLISHER
Endpapers	RV	William M. Reeves, Los Angeles	28	RV	Unknown	63	RV	Seaburg & Co., Los Angeles
ii	RV	Pacific Southwest Trust & Savings	28	WM	WHS	63	WM	Whittier Sanitary Dairy
iii	RV	CT Photochrom, Chicago	29	WM	Smith, Whittier	64	WM	Kashower
v	WM	WHS	30	DN	WHS	64	RV	Unknown
vii	RV	Cupples & Leon, NY	31	RV	Bingham	65	RV	H.S. Crocker, Los Angeles
viii	WM	WHS	31	RV	Western	65	RV	Barton
ix	RV	Cupples & Leon, NY	32	BG	Unknown	66	RV	Colourpicture, Boston
x	DN	Unknown	32	RV	Modern Pharmacy	66	WM	Barton
xi	WM	WHS	33	RV	Los Angeles Photo Postcard Co.	67	WM	WHS
xii	WM	"	33	WM	Fraishers, Inc, Pomona, CA	68	WM	Louis & Virginia Kay, Columbia
xiv	KB	Unknown	34	RV	Mitock & Sons, N. Hollywood, CA	69	WM	Barton
1	WM	WHS	34	RV	Views, Inc., Seattle	69	WM	R.E. Risher, Western
2	DN	Unknown	35	RV	Fraishers	70	RV	Wood's (Inc,) L.A.
3	RV	M. Reider, Los Angeles	35	RV	Kashower	70	RV	A.P.C.C.
3	GC	Reider	36	WM	Wyer Photo Cards, Delhi, NY	71	BG	Unknown
4	GC	"	36	RV	Columbia	71	BG	"
4	RV	Western Novelty Co., Los Angeles	37	WM	WHS	72	WM	Barton
5	WM	"	38	RV	Unknown	72	KB	Unknown
5	WM	Modern Pharmacy	39	RV	"	73	WM	Barton
6	BG	Unknown	39	RV	Reider	73	WM	"
6	BG	"	40	RV	Photochrom	74	WM	"
7	RV	Barton's, Whittier	40	RV	Reider	74	WM	The Kays, Columbia
7	WM	"	41	RV	California Sales	75	WM	WHS
8	WM	"	41	RV	Reider	76	WM	Unknown
8	WM	Unknown	42	RV	N.P.C.C., Los Angeles	77	WM	Unknown
9	WM	Barton's	42	RV	EKC (n.p.)	77	BG	Edward H. Mitchell, San Francisco
9	BG	Columbia, Hollywood	43	WM	WHS	78	RV	Reider
10	BG	"	44	RV	South Whittier School District	78	RV	"
10	BG	"	45	RV	Unknown	79	RV	Western
11	WM	WHS	45	RV	"	79	BG	Unknown
12	DN	Unknown	46	BG	Kashower	80	WM	"
13	RV	Reider	46	RV	Western	80	BG	Columbia
13	RV	Unknown	47	RV	Photochrom	81	BG	Unknown
14	WM	Reider	47	BG	Unknown	82	RV	Benham
14	BG	Benham Company, Los Angeles	48	BG	"	83	RV	California Sales, San Francisco
15	RV	Reider	48	RV	"	83	BG	Unknown
15	RV	"	49	RV	"	84	BG	Kashower
16	BG	California Sales Co., San Francisco	49	RV	"	84	RV	Reider
16	BG	Benham	50	BG	"	85	KB	L.B. Prince Co., Fairfax VA
17	BG	Modern Pharmacy	50	RV	Los Nietos School District	86	BG	Unknown
17	BG	"	51	RV	Unknown	87	WM	"
18	RV	"	51	RV	Benham	87	WM	"
18	RV	"	52	WM	Unknown	88	WM	WHS
18	GC	"	52	RV	"	88	RV	Western
19	WM	Benham	53	WM	Barton	89	BG	Photochrom
19	WM	"	53	WM	"	89	WM	Unknown
20	RV	Western	54	RV	David Rubinoff, Columbia	90	BG	"
20	BG	Douglass Caulkins, Pomona, CA	54	RV	L.A. College of Chiropractic	90	WM	WHS
21	WM	Spalding Publishing, Chicago	55	RV	Art-Tone, Des Moines, Iowa	90	WM	"
22	DN	WHS	56	RV	Whittier Hilton	91	WM	"
23	RV	Reider	57	WM	WHS	92	WM	"
23	RV	"	57	WM	"	93	KB	Rosehills Memorial Park
24	RV	CT Photochrom	58	RV	Benham	95	KB	Modern Pharmacy
24	RV	St. Bruno's Parish	58	RV	Postal Litho Colorview, Whittier			
25	RV	Neuman Postal Card Co., L.A., CA	59	WM	WHS			
25	RV	Modern	60	DN	Unknown			
26	RV	M. Kashower, Los Angeles	61	WM	WHS			
26	RV	Benham	61	BG	Kashower			
27	RV	Neuman	62	RV	Unknown			
27	RV	Los Angeles Postal Card Co.						

Symbols: RV = Author's Collection
WM = Whittier Museum Collection
BG = Bob Gardner Collection
KB = Kenny Ball Collection
DN = Dr. Nixon Collection
WHS = Whittier Historical Society

NORTH FRIEND AVENUE. WHITTIER, CAL.

THE END

This book was printed on Monza Mat paper.
The type is 10 point Century phototypeset by
Linda Gardiner with layout by Linda Gardiner,
Fernando De La Rosa and Javier De La Rosa.
The printing was done by Omar Gutierrez and the
binding by Bela Blau. The book was designed by
Rudy Valdez.